SHINE
KNOWING
SHAME

BOOKS BY MARTIN JANELLO

LIVE KNOWING LIFE
ISBN 978-0-9910649-6-0 (Paperback)
ISBN 978-0-9983020-2-7 (Kindle)

LOVE KNOWING LOVE
ISBN 978-0-9910649-7-7 (Paperback)
ISBN 978-0-9983020-3-4 (Kindle)

PINE KNOWING PAIN
ISBN 978-0-9910649-5-3 (Paperback)
ISBN 978-0-9983020-6-5 (Kindle)

SHINE KNOWING SHAME
ISBN 978-0-9983020-4-1 (Paperback)
ISBN 978-0-9983020-7-2 (Kindle)

CLIMB KNOWING AIM
ISBN 978-0-9983020-5-8 (Paperback)
ISBN 978-0-9983020-8-9 (Kindle)

KNOWING WON'T LET DARKNESS REIGN
ISBN 978-0-9983020-1-0 (Paperback)
ISBN 978-0-9983020-9-6 (Kindle)

PHILOSOPHY OF HAPPINESS
ISBN 978-0-9910649-0-8 (Hardcover)
ISBN 978-0-9910649-8-4 (Paperback, Pt. 1)
ISBN 978-0-9910649-9-1 (Paperback, Pt. 2)
ISBN 978-0-9910649-1-5 (PDF E-book)
ISBN 978-0-9910649-2-2 (Kindle)
ISBN 978-0-9910649-3-9 (EPUB)

PHILOSOPHIC REFLECTIONS
ISBN 978-0-9910649-4-6 (PDF E-book)

SHINE KNOWING SHAME

PHILOSOPHICAL QUOTES & POEMS

MARTIN JANELLO

Copyright © 2016 by Martin Janello
All rights reserved

No part of this book may be reproduced or transmitted,
in any form or by any means, electronic,
mechanical, or otherwise,
without prior written permission from its
copyright owner

Cover, book design, and artwork by Martin Janello

Published by Palioxis Publishing

Palioxis, Palioxis Publishing,
and the Palioxis Publishing colophon
are trademarks owned by Martin Janello

Publisher website:
www.palioxis.com

Book website:
www.philosophyofhappiness.com

ISBN 978-0-9983020-4-1

First Edition

CONTENTS

I. WISDOM	1
II. DEFENSE AND PRETENSE	19
III. FAILURE	43
IV. ENDS AND BEGINNINGS	63
V. SOUNDS AND VISIONS	87
VI. PASSION	105
VII. CHAOS AND CLARITY	139
VIII. REMEMBRANCE	163
IX. STORIES	181
X. OUT AND WITHIN	205

This book is dedicated

to

those who

grow to shine

beyond their shame

I.
WISDOM

I. WISDOM

should we wonder

what is wrong with someone

who's warm without apparent reason

we ought to ask

what is wrong with us

separation

is the

original sin

what often first

stands in our way

is our opinion

of ourselves

she said a good day's
when the right parts
are hurting

why should we care
if the weak don't make it
when all in nature's directed that way
because arrogance is our weakness

take heart
in your heart
and keep ownership
mind your mind
and keep independence

I. WISDOM

before you show anger

are cold or careless

avenge attack

or take advantage

before you hurt

your innate loving spirit

take a step back and consider

being gracious

when others are not

is most what grace is about

being what we claim to be

implies a constant struggle

canvas paint brush
hand mind inspiration
audience critic
all one
we must be

Try to avoid those who take
friendliness as a weakness. Most of
all, do not adjust to them.

the sole reason
humans can('t) live
with each other
is an unaware mind

I. WISDOM

high bred monkeys
with cars and smart phones

we keep looking
for easy ways out
when there is no escape

carelessness of ignorant people
tends to define our conditions

good for no reason
some people make a life of it

knowing is only a temporary state
till we know enough
to question our knowledge

travel together
while you do your things
don't ask or accept
major sacrifices

being with you
should be raptured elevation
for someone who's loving you back
working on this is a dutiful art
applied in due course to every heart

I. WISDOM

people who think
things are out to get them
will often do the honors themselves

not caring who cares
must be done sometimes
but mostly we should
practice harmony

the minutes
the hours
the decades we miss
if we are not careful
our life will be this

Sacrificing yourself for others is
supremely selfish because it causes
enduring torture from inability to
repay you unless others sacrifice
themselves as well.

damages we all do to each other
thinking we are wise
humbleness is the virtue supreme

let this day live my dear
its brevity carry no fear
our history stay clear
and no thought spent on tomorrow

I. WISDOM

the best we can hope for

is not not to fade

but finding someone

who will do it with us

most people prefer

what is rare

having no sense

for abundant love

we fuss about life's receipts

from inception

but there are no warranties

nor returns

an arc connects our first thought
through pastime to our last
life came and went too fast

be wary of those eager to connect
in one-way communications

do not fall
for numbing your mind
we're made to feel pain for a reason

no good reason to ration love

I. WISDOM

something unsaid about
keeping your cake
is that it will spoil
if not eaten

being human
finally means
taking exception
to implied fate

Happiness has to do with
coincidence, as its root implies. But
another part is derived from making
things happen.

happiness craves

expanding one's senses

instead of hindering them

we exist

to help one another

to live work and die

in bliss and peace

moving thereby

toward humankind's purpose

in two hundred years

most we're fretting about

will be un or recycled trash

I. WISDOM 15

to be whole
surround yourself
with people
responding to kindness

history's made
by insanely obnoxious
the rest of us try
to keep things together

Ask yourself who might be interested
to prevent you from developing your
own philosophy of a happy life, and
for what purpose.

many who lowered their head
to be knighted
have been beheaded instead

everyone is our teacher
though we might learn
unintended lessons

our life is permeated by strings
they pull us but also give structure

crudeness never expresses strength

I. WISDOM

go resolute
and do it your way
soon you'll regret
leaving love behind

The health of a relationship is
measurable by how much you can
stay yourself, and by how much you
try to adjust another.

no heart of gold would be so bold
as to judge the value of people
its courage to encourage instead
won't let its goodness get to its head

life will probably not get better
until we make it so

the you and the me
of this realm are unreal

wisdom of flowers
spring is coming

don't send your heart
it might not come back
if addressees won't return it

II.
DEFENSE
AND
PRETENSE

II. DEFENSE AND PRETENSE

they keep us like children
fed warm and busy
so we won't reflect
on their rule in a tizzy

she had a problem
with being polite
to silently hurt
to not hurt another

we claim giving up
is not an option
while all the while sensing
how close it is

her pride kept
getting in the way
of anything
to be proud of

pretty girls
often shielded from truth
by men who lie
lying in waiting

we don't care much
to think or feel
all we're consuming
has done that for us

II. DEFENSE AND PRETENSE

how much of panache
is being at odds
and going to lengths
not to show it

say what you want to caution me
a whish of her locks
a flush of her lips
a flash of her eyes
throws all to the wind

deathly afraid of reality's questions
we spin it to knots and nets
holding up answers

Most do not want to explore why we are here, what here is, and how to react, fearing the answers or the inability to find any.

a time when we listen
to loudmouths
to drown out the pains
of our inner voices

how i am
is a rude inquisition
leaving me showed
you don't care anymore

II. DEFENSE AND PRETENSE

the lie becomes truth
if we lower our hurt
by going along with power

she suspects she
could have any man
hooked flapping on her line
that's why she's so careful
not giving any sign

never threaten
a lover to leave
extortion will not
beget what you need

no one can put forth
an even keel for long
without being held at night

i feel you want to go
and try not to let you know
that i always lie
about wanting you free
maybe oh baby
that's why you're leaving me

drowning in predictable muck
she thought she could not
remove from her being

II. DEFENSE AND PRETENSE

she always had him catering
insisting it payment
that she'd be a client

here's to the lies
that keep up our lives

she calls him an artist
as if a disease
a quirky oddball who puts up a piece
a humored child with disgraces rife
an uncouth zealot full of strife
to be kept at a distance
from her ordered life

don't be a victim
and if you are
know others assuring
you won't remain

but you won't see me
and though you do
you're scared of me
i'm too much like you

where and with whom
and how you are
i don't dare ask
as much as it kills me

II. DEFENSE AND PRETENSE

you state what you claim to be
tight from the getgo
as if you fear someone
will question that

people with lacking control
may try to compensate
by exerting it over others
or worshiping it in others

mostly pretending
life won't be ending
acting surprised
when it does

using others as stepping stones
choking their lives
and crushing their bones
they call it getting ahead

her penchant
for the overly dramatic
made him hold back even more

tedium slows time
causing wait for its passing
some prefer that
so their life seems extended
getting an edge on forever beyond

II. DEFENSE AND PRETENSE

she hates to think
like everybody
unless they think
the way she thinks

not good enough
at sight unseen
obsessed
with judging herself
through others

she calls me a man
as if it could keep me
from ever being her friend

some men feign toughness
in compensation
for their natural state
of deflation

the beautiful dolls
get all the applause
their movers and shapers
stay back for their cause

he goes for who says it
not what is said
looks for what someone is
ignoring trait

II. DEFENSE AND PRETENSE

she's afraid
to be nakedly honest
among a mob
raping clothed with deceit

the hard and the soft
are roles and reversals
but in the end
we're boned watery flesh

to warrant inclusion
attendance and pay
patrons may sway themselves
liking the play

many build shells
around themselves
to travel unscathed
through life's many hells
the valiant go naked of armor

she is afraid of him
taxing her life
with not much in return

he pleaded with her
why do you claim me
if wanting to love you
is reason to shame me

II. DEFENSE AND PRETENSE

we are flowers

sometimes thinking we are rocks

we love calm light

seeking friends in storm and night

to not be afraid anymore

wondering what's wrong

with all these people

how can they live with their sternity

charlatan's empires

built on fear

and telling people

what they want to hear

she needed his love
to be sacrificed cruelly
on her bloodstained virgin
altar of pride

holding so much in reserve
saving soul expressions
for days which continued
will likely never come

she held back unsure
that being with him
could make up the pain
of his absence

II. DEFENSE AND PRETENSE

she does not want love
but love keeps wanting
to take her existence hostage

she plead temporary insanity
love ought not need such humiliation

most of us do not want our freedom
because it deprives us
of certainty's safety

what if we had no tolerance for liars

he acts like he'd like
to catch her attention
but then he's afraid
what to do with it

we choose to root for teams
who don't know us
would we not rather have teams
who know us rooting for us

i'll try to look better
behave more to like me
now that love
has me under our guns

II. DEFENSE AND PRETENSE

pretentiousness worn ironically
like cowboy boots
on her marzipan feet

i thought i felt
i had the impression
most sorries start like that
time to come off
our minds' high horses
and walk through life without a hat

i want the real
even if it's not
what i want

how can it be
that men chase or flee
not stand their ground
till peace is found
their death blood life
a bond to ban strife

she's busy making people buy
into her fierce self-admiration
pays tokens no attention or tribute

thick shells
become encumbering encasements
once we decide to move about freely

II. DEFENSE AND PRETENSE

thoughts of us
seeds that stay
over-protected
cursed to decay

don't hiss dissing this
your mind
the forked tongue
of an angry curled heart

the first thing
she told me was prejudiced
as if to protect her
from being mistaken

she never had hands
upon her before
and flinched from the comfort
his touch meant to give

indifference and ill will
kill tender parts of us
trusting we'll be quiet
pretending not to be hurt

we deem the sun is rising
when our ground is turning
and keep this way surmising
with neighbors' houses burning

III.
FAILURE

III. FAILURE

the hell we make for
ourselves and others
devils aspiring to be angels
or cynics believing no god bothers

two causes
we fall short of expectations
lack of knowhow
and right mix of motivations

some people some animals
won't respond accordingly
they're on another frequency
or may be wired differently

tell them our prayers
their misery will end
all that we look for
is absolution

ignorant pride
of a made-up woman
her cats will charm her
when everything fails

you make assumptions
i do not meet
i am messy
and you want neat

III. FAILURE

you are icing on my cookie
but your sweetness makes me puky

a world that is heavily sedated
when it should have been at peace

collapsing tents
with sad clowns

times you can't help think
what would have happened
are my consolations of pain

a flower unseen

a woman unloved

a shoe unscuffed

a jewel unbuffed

a life unbeen

beautiful dreams

and pretty flowers

left at your door

that remains unopened

his life seemed like

a basket filled

with crumpled discarded ideas

III. FAILURE

she's nastiest
to the ones who love her
knowing she's safe with them
in her abuse

with her he could not
hear himself think
no use she had
his life figured out

we and other sinister powers
point us toward windows
against which we fly
until we drop and die

look baby
he's an options trader
and you are asking
for life long commitment

her resentment
of being ignored
makes them abstain
for unjust reason

love's tragedy
is the rift between
promise of intention
and reality

III. FAILURE

what would it take

he keeps guessing

nothing he has

most distressing

she longed for him

to undress her heart

he only thought of clothes falling

arrested in caskets

of boards hinting safety

life's pleasures are dying to resurrect

still mostly we're worried

'bout acting correct

many of us have lived their extent
and it's just now a matter of time

she drew on him
to give her love
not realizing
he needed it too

she broke his stride
complained he can't dance
throttled his throat
denounced he won't sing
ripped out his heart
and claimed he can't love

III. FAILURE

words he wanted
were missing
and she would not help
to find them

you can paint
say sing scream all you want
the world's moved on
to prepackaged confections

like thin piano wire
grating through my soul
its parts together
still lethally severed

conditioned to care
to be better than others
instead of being
more helpful to them

romantic love
makes regret
the enemy

life's question marks
we don't correctly answer
turn into hooks
suspending our progress
or tearing us down

III. FAILURE

meeting requirements
instead of people

he thought she was takeout dinner
abiding by ritualistic debt

making lovers stay
there is no such thing
but one can make them go away

she got cold feet
but allowed him to warm them

defining saints
as kind even-minded
we give ourselves
easy passes to fail

when we crave nights or days
to save us from the other
our balance is asunder
and we try not to crash

too much of her
has already left
to make him believe
she's still with him

III. FAILURE 57

a gentleman
a modern knight
strong honorable gracious
she seeks among losers
crawling the night

my angel has flown
i grasp at feathers
sinking in the still

with high expectations
to be struck by lightning
she would not give
gentle love a chance

she's thirsty for him
grown up to be ice
he cannot be like water

right she agreed
when he told her
he loved her

poetries stark
like broken trees
twisted by gales for nothing
sentiments dark
recited with glee
that others share our suffering

III. FAILURE 59

most people refuse
to really live
until it is time to die

feeling both guilty and debt to him
by association with his transgressions
she makes an arrangement with sin

though she only whined
he had no compunctions
agreeing with whatever she said
she had a listener
and he was unctuous
single minded to get her to bed

staying where love dwells not enough
generates most of our pain
trying to force it by battling the rough
makes us be vain in vain

earth's drag of sadness
continues its slowdown
not enough love left
to go around

locked in a self-admiring trance
of being published and academic
the poet decided to forgo the chance
of realizing his work was anemic

III. FAILURE

eager poet deemed his life's duty

casting in words

the essence of beauty

he tried to describe her

but soon could see

it would end in utter catastrophe

some people's kindness

should come with notice

that it is not a sample

humankind's on

the back of its heels

still we go faster to nowhere

good he said

now she was leaving

luck would have soon run out anyway

not since he had gained

emotional recall

was need

for emptiness

raging more

mountains of words exchanged

upheavals insults and dramatics

all this commotion yields

silent lone bitter fanatics

IV.
ENDS
AND
BEGINNINGS

IV. ENDS AND BEGINNINGS

life is like toothpaste
after we step on it
'xcept that we may get some refills

nothing will be
like this again
welcoming or
regretting that
prefaces our happiness

you was this
she says
i agree with her grammar
more definitely gone like that

sometimes we only can blank
and go on
and baby it's one of those days
can't tell which one of us has won
both maybe in each our ways
but it's goodbye to something

take me away from me someone
i'll gladly go to stop the pain

he is an iser
she is a waser
how can a will be
arise from their union

IV. ENDS AND BEGINNINGS

being in love
is so overwhelming
she feels her life's bearings
are coming unhinged

some cowards don't dare
to walk away
they stay until time
will pass them

mostly i was
but how much i will be
is up to me
i hope

today i will restring

my old guitar

replacing tired oxidized wire

with shiny coiled pouncing fire

young god

she says

i was

i was

i was

i know i will get over you

it's me getting over you

i can't get over

IV. ENDS AND BEGINNINGS

my hearts are beating
in all of life
each birth each death
my renewal and killing

night moth i was
not being too bright
since turned away
you are not sun's light
beat myself up for nothing

nature's division
and convergence
available in us

she took off her shoes
and walked to the wild
i know she is here now
to hunt life with me

i don't care i will always love you
even though you don't want me to
run along and let me be love
hoping one day you will find it too

never mind that they are all gone
they were in reality never here
the one who will stay is yet to come
in time though so have another beer

IV. ENDS AND BEGINNINGS

she cannot wait for him anymore
clocks ticking muffled by silence
she wants to know
what she's living for
his tight embrace seems like violence

it's all artificial
she sadly said
go back to real fire
to bake real bread

no don't stay
and emotions will show
the path to you more clearly

today i ran out
of all my rhyme
i had to get away
and had you know
the mood i'm in
nothing more to say
and no more wasting time

must i be
i'd rather not
without you

go on
she just won't

IV. ENDS AND BEGINNINGS

change now after all
it's possible still
if you will your being to it

she had me going
until i arrived
she had me dying
until i survived

water nails
clang on icy rails
at the shoreline promenade
where she stands pondering
joining the sea

we always have the choice
to be mournful over time lost
or eager about days to come
selecting will direct our life

colton is an odd name for a wife
but this is what she chose
for her new life
if she goes

the manner and tone
in which you say you
makes me expect
something ravishing new

IV. ENDS AND BEGINNINGS

tell me this craziness
will it end
when all i say do or don't
seems to offend
you have no reason to judge me

he said he would die
without her with him
but she had given that
consideration

so many bemoan
they can't stand their life
without being willing to change it

new morning hope
had left him lately
wounded by demons
he called upon daily

she questioned in strife
is this love yet
as if sitting back
for it to arrive

frequently people
who should be dead
are some of the ones
who seem most alive

IV. ENDS AND BEGINNINGS

at the end of our life
we should get courageous
instead of resigning ourselves

merging your beings
to make someone new
who brings out the best
and the worst in you

go away
why
because i must stay
and we will not ever
do well together

keep me going

or keep going

he danced heavily like a bear

until she stretched

his mind's sinews to heaven

forgive that

yes move on

too much has not happened

for us to part or stay

IV. ENDS AND BEGINNINGS

she cannot stand to be with him
while she is lying down
trust has not taken that corner yet
since he came around

sometimes
when crossing paths with strangers
a voice inside begs
stop
love
don't let go

she was some arbitrary stranger
who made me believe in destiny

last night i had just met you
with all prospects new
of what you could be
and not encountered your sad true
that you're beginning to let me see
you say you don't want to burden me
but what chance of love have i if i flee

be a flower
and butterflies
will return

to find peace
we must have open eyes

IV. ENDS AND BEGINNINGS

go on he said
i'll sit here just listening
until you start work
on fulfilling your prayers

proclaiming the times
for talk and song over
she turned to me
with intention to act

you easily draw me
out of my shall
and give in
to whims of maybe

la rosée d'une fleur
renouvelle chaque matin

the dew of a flower
renews every morning

the advantage of being written off
is the chance to write our own story

what to do
when you can't stand
at your station any longer
expecting a train
that may never come

IV. ENDS AND BEGINNINGS

those awful caterpillars

gnawing your heart

until it almost dies

one day become butterflies

filling it with

sun-warmed softly batting wings

often it's tough

not to fade away

not to give up

when we know

pain will stay

and resisting

means hell to pay

still we hold on

to a fragile ray

boy who was tutored

to be parents' martyr

while other children

played field and water

girl who was warned

not to soil her dress

finally run to create their own mess

What a world it would be if we all
showed a little more of us - and found
we are not alone wanting to dance in
the moonlight.

courage always lives with fear

IV. ENDS AND BEGINNINGS

you told me your story
and i told you mine
continued together
at least for some time

mow down the flowers
delusioned you win
next year they'll bloom again

i mourn losing touch
with you old friend
let us forget
we did not care
for a while

she felt like

her soulmate had died

or stopped looking

lovely flowed freely

when you cared

to join me

silently resting

on edge at deep waters

you know it's in the midst of fights

that we must affirm we are loved

if we stay tight-lipped entire nights

slowly this light becomes snuffed

V. SOUNDS AND VISIONS

V. SOUNDS AND VISIONS

colors and sparks
her eyes were changing
drinking deep love's
endless sky and sea

do i still believe
my life will be glorious
as when i was young
looking out to my self

The vulnerable honesty of a poem
connects the souls of its creator and
reader. It thus forms an essential tool
of emotional communication.

stuck in caged morasses
makes hard to sing of flying
then again it's all some have

i write my best
but then i rest
most of your loveliness
cannot be spoken

dream of a byzantine city
shared lights and delights
of long-faded beings
leaving them mornings
i too share their death

V. SOUNDS AND VISIONS

none of the angels wore wingtips

grownups displaying
directness like children
banned from societies' make-believe

where are the forests
where fairies danced
or at least our imaginations

when the heart sings
all the earth rings

i write my poetry at night
with nobody listening but i

don't tell me this is our song
because we'll get sick of it some day

Consciousness is a neural network's
awareness of separateness from
observations.

good poetry is a stirring
to the wind chimes of our minds

V. SOUNDS AND VISIONS

the poem proved
a bridge too far
he fell through a ceiling
while reaching its star

in musical landscapes
of wallpaper patterns
it's almost a relief to hit our shin
on an ankle biting coffee table

he wants to go back
to hearing the music
that years ago stopped
playing in his heart

in wayward dreams
she is still with him
doing the things
she left him for

she doesn't understand
my music
too loud
too weird
too everything

the leaves were this color
that you would not know
since you only look at them fallen

we think that we know how to live
because we watch it on the screen
we just don't get around to it
because we watch it on the screen

what if machine guns
sang happy tunes
instead of screaming
attackattackattack

the smell of
undead fish and sun
clean sand
washed every fifteen seconds

he wondered how sun
would taste on his tongue
or rains felt in his veins
if toes were roots
and fingers were leaves
and life and nature were one

A good song for me starts with words
and their meanings - to which I then
give more aural expression.

i know all is one but i am not done
paddling hard to get in the flow
that's what i need to focus on

V. SOUNDS AND VISIONS

his life's goal was
to manifest love
so when he died
it would still carry on

you are if i go
that's all i want
because i'll be in your mind

guitars won't sing
without strings attached
hearts in a fling
are in a way matched
carrying reverberations

listening to cuts
of many years back
embedded they open again

i often think
where mankind would be
if no one were willing
to fight one another

your folds unfold
to let me dream on steel
i know now bed
why you have rolls
but not a steering wheel

V. SOUNDS AND VISIONS

how can i not sing
of my love for her
and live it every day
she makes me
so much better a man
than ever i hoped to pray

the moon made me rise
and want to be wise
about our life and love

some day we'll sing
to different moons and suns
entrusting them with similar wants

he never knew

whether falling silent

or jumping right in

was what beauty called for

few feelings as raw

as a plugged-in guitar

to play with her tension

share screaming attack

feeding back

to the hair on my neck

my heart cannot read

it just looks at pictures

my poems come with pictures
but i try to build them
in readers' minds

la lune est le fond
d'une bougie allumée

the moon is the bottom
of a lit candle

To me, Beethoven is the father of
rock. His is the first music that
aspires to and benefits from being
played on "eleven."

spare me the drama

he thought in the theater

i'm merely here to be seen

blameless you are

for craving escape

fairy tale dreams

and visions of beauty

yet soon return

and face the ugly

lest you be eaten by life

poetry is a dance of words

dance poetry without them

V. SOUNDS AND VISIONS

not all poetry

is spun gold

some is more

like string cheese

Before one can write worthwhile poetry, one must understand the difference between imagination and pretense.

some guitars

resemble women

this one's a blonde

in tight black leather pants

In poetry, we must resist the
temptation to assume that
mellifluous words equal truth.

dreaming her say
i'll be there
when you need me
i cannot wait
to wake knowing that

you follow my fingers
play the baby grand
what i play next
is in your mind and hand

VI.
PASSION

VI. PASSION

what i've been through
and then came you
white eyes
with sharp flannel funnels

and though i may leave
to gain the world
i always come back
to win your heart

though we are joined
i hardly know you
please keep revealing
yourself to me

the loveliest writs

i muster

lose luster

in your presence

your favorite flower

is baby's breath

and i'm not afraid

to know it

don't tell me

reasons you love me

for i would then fear

they'd pass before me

VI. PASSION

say something deep about her ways
without scaring her by implying
my heart angels urged and no lying
so i let her know how in my case
she brightens even sunny days

i'm ready she trilled
and filled me with doubt
should we go
or stay harmonizing

i know you're not listening
you watch the glistening
of her lips pout

the best

and worst days

were seeing her

how much he'd like

to spread his wings

to shield her

from incoming fire

and how pathetic

this passion rings

in foil over sticks and wire

more than mine

i want you to be yours

VI. PASSION

some girls will not let you forget
that they gave themselves freely
trying to hold you in eternal debt
turning love's juicy peach mealy

she does not need clothes
to hold things in place
this is what she knows
and what he prays

lost
could it be
he was fond of her
past all horizons known

that she would touch him

without demands

how someone touchable

would have to be

i love this room

of our gentle fire

reflecting soul shadows

for us to read

pressing themselves

against each other

brought forth the essence

of love everlasting

VI. PASSION

you must not
give up to him too soon
or he will feel
incapable hunting

a woman will let you do
anything to her
if she trusts you
but honoring her trust
will prevent you

i like that you're foreign
i've had familiar
it's where my dreams went to winter

i love the manner
you're moving your hair
more since i know
you do it for me

she cries with me
when i am tormented
that's why i nevermore
want to be sad

do not direct him
trust let him be man
you will win
stirring his passion again

VI. PASSION

she warps time
just walking by
people dream
stare smile and sigh
her aura's gleaming
all clichés apply
she is incarnate love

don't follow baby
how it could be
that out of all the guys
you're wanting me
you say i'm special
but i fail to see
what in that specialty
would turn your key

at times i think
it would be a relief
accepting what never will be
but then a voice questions
how do you know

cute she calls him
not what he went for
still he's disarmed and charmed

just like there are lights
that are whiter than white
you give delights
a pen cannot write

VI. PASSION

you say i am dangerous
for unleashing you

she doesn't think
my jokes are funny
she humors them
like a nanny a child
but drops her reserve
when i whisper honey
ready for bedlam
or something else wild

love's work is draining us each day
nights we seek frantically restoration

the various ways

she says come on

astound me without end

taking her time

puts on serious debt

years she can never retrieve

only forestalled by

his loyal commitment

and hope love lends him reprieve

the most significant step of true love

is granting power

to turn us on or off to life

VI. PASSION

your hemlines
skirt my face
like grazing razors

contemplative playing softly
while rain is falling
worshiping your skin
cut by the ring
of the stupid phone

ratcheting up
is what she's good at
riding her loops
is his favorite thrill

she doesn't respect him
for waiting at her door
except for guarding it sometimes

this one is driving
to break the stick shift
that one is polishing chrome
till i'm home

if i went to the end of the known
would you go with me
if i would dare losing
by choosing the edge
would you ride it with me

VI. PASSION

i am unclothed
for you to see
this is my body confined
but unlimited love
for you to set free

closed-eyed
she's exploring me
wanting to know how i feel

your smile
caresses my ailing soul
your heat
enflames my waiting coal

how come you like me
so much you cry
but then you don't want me
to soothe you

we walked to the lily pond
laughing and naked
the moonlight had shown
more than silhouettes' charm

i knew i had changed
and grown quite up
when i did not mind
that she licked my ice cream

VI. PASSION

you
i do not like to say that word
it is too separate from me
have taken over all my world
except that i still feel whole and free

she praises i know
how women feel
but only because they make me

you say touch me
but i won't budge
hovering close
is making you crazy

l'heure bleue

your warm sentiments

and mine

switching from tea

to red savage wine

she disassembled me

letters of phrases

artfully spun together once

hold it close

but not too tight

i'd like to keep

this feeling alive

VI. PASSION

why he complained
must i dream of her
i don't know even who she is

our tears fell into each other's eyes

rapt up
in your hideaway
heavy sensual overload

pull envelop pierce and streak me
skin tight fusion you secrete me

like your life
treat a work of art

let her breathe freely
then take it for a while

we give too much away for free
but that's how we are - indelibly

i know i'm not enough for her
but she makes me more
of what i need to give

VI. PASSION

warrior i am
mars is my planet
i will defend your soft
feeling my strength

sometime soon
or eventually later
he will lose faith
in your tepid soul

holding her close
has lost its promise
for letting her go
is invariably next

she says again

she wants me to touch her

trembling

yet it is not fear anymore

she dreamt of fires

and floods of emotions

earths shaking

and gales pounding

all during elements of accounting

the complex design

served to remind him

it's lingerie not lungerie

VI. PASSION

back lit hair
gives her the flair
of a flame-tinged angel
love or ire
i'm in awe of this fire

sometimes he makes her
wanting to die
because he's her reason for living

the truth about her
she is poetry
all descriptions
copies stolen

he knew it was love
when mentions of her
burned brand-like
but also warmed his heart

the embarrassment
of being shot down
was nothing compared
to the torture
of not being able to land

promise me
you will not die again
even if love has you bleeding

VI. PASSION

in love our belief
is a tender flower
we proclaim invincible

lost in nocturne
embracing lovers

she uses words
like dawdling
drawling them gently
in her exquisite mouth
she is from georgia evidently
and i after hearing her
want to go south

the devil if real
would lead you to love

their relationship was proof
cold fusion can be accomplished

these braids
in which she wears her hair
leave me hopelessly entangled

life seems too long for longing
and short for a few days elation

VI. PASSION

the worst fate in love
is missing someone
who keeps on aware of this
playing with us

dreams i once knew
seem stale and won't do
now that i breathed
the presence of you

the most ravishing girl
without even trying
launched my heart in a whirl
and scrambled my wiring

after the sizzle

she puts on an apron

to satisfy his need for beacon

dancing round splatter

fryin' chicken nude

he moves close to her

not thinking of food

what's this love good for

elated with you

but paying the price when I'm not

affliction of damage and cure will do

more harm than a slow lonely rot

VI. PASSION

she liked his strong hands
attending her skin
as if they were sculpting wet clay

don't fool yourself thinking
love easily ends
some go through much pain to kill it

she says no and i'm sick with dread
foolish to think
she'd go out with me
love must have messed up my head
but now she says come
to my place instead

she's wilding my drive
i was stuck in first gear

she admits i tamed her
but that's not what i want

she reminds me
of fruit at its peak

skimming his lips
with two fingers
she had kissed

VI. PASSION

takes my drive for reckless spins
dizzying speed 'round her curves
no brakes or steering still she wins
the prize of my heart she deserves

she and i are
like water and fire
merging converging
to hot scalding steam

Romantic love unites in and out of body experiences. It is when we live our most because it grants us access to bliss we did not know existed.

you know or you will

that life has no mercy

we only can beat it

by blunt force of hearts

come on she said

come on love me to tears

make me forget

when they fell

in your absence

if it weren't for your mouth

i might have well lost my taste

for love

VII. CHAOS AND CLARITY

VII. CHAOS AND CLARITY

driftwood we are
tumbling on a shore
will we burn
in someone's fire

not sure i like the power of words
with threatened falsity and violation
yes all tools have dark sides
but these can directly form minds

letting things take their courses
taught him to blame himself
just as he would have
had he tried to change them

given enough motivation
the human brain
can rationalize anything
this is where the heart comes in

he thinks the reasons why she left
would only have relevance
had she stayed

to know what happened
is often as difficult as
guessing what will happen
emotional theories abound
and rationalizations gloss over

VII. CHAOS AND CLARITY

like birds in a house
of mirrors we are
sitting still bruised afraid of flight

don't know really why i cry
and i'm not really crying
it's just that i let myself
realize feelings
unfiltered and without lying

borrowed hope
on a stranger's ticket
she does not know
if she wants to go

she says i seem to her
pretty normal
i don't know if i want this praise

so wondered why
they would
or would not love me
each choice
incomprehensible
and clear at times

intentions clear
retreat hate or fear
are oddly estranged derelictions

VII. CHAOS AND CLARITY

it's not that we're sleeping
but we're not awake
life has us too tired
to put up a fight
it's not that we're trembling
but we're not at peace
life has us too scared
to follow the light

your lips promise cherry kisses
or is it spits of pits

she said i can no more recognize
but had she paid attention before

don't know if i could
if she let me go
or remain if she begged
don't know if i like
that she needs me so
or care if i got wrecked

we did not come here
for popular reasons
just to speak the truth

all i want is honesty
to a fault of hurting me
but you won't let it get to that

VII. CHAOS AND CLARITY

morning haze
dreams solving maze
i am geborgen
anew in our love

dreamless stupor
when we are awake
flashes of consciousness
is it too late

is this what you want
i should be doing
you guide my hand
will my mind stay free

waves of stupidity
threaten to drown us
giving up thinking
so we can feel good

democracy is
the agreed right of a majority
to govern a minority
don't mistake it for freedom

it's only still me
because there is you
at least sometimes
when i'm searching

VII. CHAOS AND CLARITY

don't know anymore
if i ever did
the pieces of me
if they ever fit
together to make me whole

was anything you
or was it the hue
of morn ambers
imbued with hope

crazed demands for adulation
poppies in bloom
know it's over soon

she is soul searching
but dares not succeeding
only the drinking
can keep her sane

once ignorant what loomed out there
reeling hard when sadness hit
world of impurity made him feel dirty
he could not wash his hands of it

sometimes the best is yet to go
or might have already left
a blessing is that we don't know
so we can with some hope rest

VII. CHAOS AND CLARITY

the moment she let him
touch her breast
she knew immediately
if he'd pass muster

the freezer
left ajar on vacation
taught him
the frangible nature of life

Poetic contemplation and sensitivity are at times mistaken for frailty and sadness when they really express the courage and joy of awareness.

the rare sense

of presence

in our essence

what is

space time matter consciousness

we only know

what we dare to believe

without being proven wrong

suspense in mid air

gives us a scare

that hearts and minds

might be overflowing

VII. CHAOS AND CLARITY

frightening bouts of consciousness
make us sink back to obliviousness

she reached through the wall
and offered her hand
but he only feared
she'd be grabbing

waking up
to a day without time
just sunbathed air
and my life with you
sit here with me dear
while our hearts shine

specs on a flying rolling ball
with grandiose grounding illusions

idiots will buy dieting tips
from an overweight famous person

paring down to what we need
brings our self to light

you tell me you're mine
and i think you mean
you are not anyone else's

VII. CHAOS AND CLARITY

at times she still gives me

refreshing notions

she'll never be a downright sure thing

the ultimate problem

we don't know why

we're here in either direction

weakening us to suggestion

loves dressing up and facing the day

throwing it all off at night

nestling into a bath

over-sized shirt

soft gurgling music and me

she wants certainty

he could and would defend her

though he may never have to

had i forgotten

how good life could be

or did i ever know

these are moot points now

with your loving me

and the mind you blow

he carried calm assuredness

his amity would one day attract

a trusting wild soul from the thicket

don't tell me
you like butterflies
but can't stand caterpillars

love is tricky
because we fear
to need or be needed
too little or much

the best ahead
now apparent to me
upon giving up on her
or am i just talking up a bet
after a past hard to bear

the most blessed
and desperate thought is
i'll die not having known this

holding loved ones very close
won't let us get a good look at them
maybe that is how blind love survives

see my eyes
they look for you
feel my hands
they reach for you
meet my soul
it longs for you

VII. CHAOS AND CLARITY

she wore a flower in her hair
that signaled
she did
and did not care

living presumptuously and arranged
resisting to be proven wrong
lost since we were children

walking with her
did she say
you'll like me
or rather you're like me
and why do i think it matters

my love for you
may not be much
but it always will be
as much i can love

hung-over haze
punch-drunk from her ways
reality forces his gaze
into a searing blaze

don't know why
she does not speak
or is it me not hearing
have we left each other's range

VII. CHAOS AND CLARITY

why do you never smile at me
cause love my dear
is a serious business

easy to get wrapped up in ugly
it lingers and lurches everywhere
she steadfastly pleads
the power of beauty
i trust it will win
because she is there

am i still here
or is it only
that you keep thinking of me

she takes my hand
placing it on her chest
even before we kiss
you hold my heart
and i cannot rest
till you know where it is

cold winter days ahead
i like the idea of
not being diverted

having been left to his devices
he was inundated
by thoughts not his own

VIII.
REMEMBRANCE

VIII. REMEMBRANCE

dreams of all kinds
fade without fail
but poems of you stay
etched in the walls
of my mind's halls

he keeps cooking dinners
he won't eat
as if they could make her
come back and stay home

her life had flat-lined
with startling blips
recalling her potentials

why do i so vividly recall the luck
of inconsequential moments
when we turned beside
that eighteen wheel truck

you think
the indians we killed
did not have little girls
waiting for daddy to come home

most people i knew
did not die from old age
they simply got tired
of senseless living

VIII. REMEMBRANCE

you did not mind
to follow the band
our castle was marked
by a two person tent
one month that touring summer

i did not find
you were for rent
including your heart
and your morals were bent
till i caught you with our drummer

can't say i don't miss you
not only as muse
the times when i kissed you
were worth the abuse
but i lost my best friends
to living the blues

night sweat fueled fires
in marish locked spires
from which they try rise
in the mornings
evil won't let them peacefully rest

faded photographs of us
that cannot be retaken

not enough booze in the cabinet
to make her go on and finally forget
she'll carry these wounds
of lost love around bleeding
smearing her life till she's dead

VIII. REMEMBRANCE

we're only as good
as the last thing we stated
no one remembers beyond

back road mountain pass we passed
embalmed in clouds
primordially muffled
our universe focused
trajectories suspended
you did not want to stay

how do you love a heart
bruised to its core
that mistrusts its own hurtful beating

it's late at night
and she won't let him
change history
even going forward

she called boys hey
until deciding
if it made sense
remembering their name

he wants to return
to when he was feeling
emotions recounted now
for the first time

VIII. REMEMBRANCE

you have me return to a lost october
the city was stage to our play
then you wrapped your angel's wings
in a pullover
and left me bereft of more lines to say

when people die
we recite some phrases
and wonder if their voice
should have been recorded

holiday moon
hollow promises
gone too soon

sunlight through

the back of her ear

made me remember

how she was dear

color of rosy piglet

comet coursing

to never return

she took a shine at me

on her way to burn

scraping on bones

their ancestors left

unable to forget them

VIII. REMEMBRANCE

she could not evoke
the ardors stirred then
except for faintly
the hearsay of them

when i was small
i thought spring blooms
were for my birthday
and thanked them all

he recalled youth's mornings
of fresh baked bread
enjoying it buttered
fore health warnings' dread

mostly she told me
she was just tired
warding off worries
without reward

i recall a city
you've never been to
but i roamed its streets
forlorn looking for you

as you stepped out of bed this morn
and walked in horizontal light
you carried the glow of a saintly form
an image exposing still in my mind

VIII. REMEMBRANCE

it was a time
when words meant more
when people gave theirs
or cursed another's fortune
when one could not say
i love you and not mean it

knowing you were
trusting you are
wishing you'll always be there

impressions of life kept creeping back
as waiting halls in temporary stations
or trains with uncertain destinations

she hated him deadly
with silent passion
for stirring up memories
of her frustrations
he knew but suspected
love still had a chance

how quietly you come and go
dead figment
of my heart's encrusted routine

crestfallen to me
was the tritest cliché
till you made me suffer its meaning

VIII. REMEMBRANCE

i often think back to autumn days
when our love's spring was found
nature's alive now
in unnerving praise
loud consolations abound

i know that i should write her now
and yet forgot what to say about how
it got so complicated

after a while his memory merged
with lies he reread in mail
details slowly replaced by myth
shelved love preserves going stale

she took him on a rousing flight
through fragrant soft-petaled trees
dropping him suddenly yet in spite
he's reminiscing the breeze

she remembered
once being unguarded
toward feelings that then
crashed like breakers on her

inconsolable or demure
running from shadows
or hiding in them
light is the only cure

VIII. REMEMBRANCE

chivalry loyalty trust and grace
have become superseded ways
under the rigors of profit
leaving us poorer of it

she jeers at me
i've seen you before
as if i had ruined her vision

tries not thinking
of life with him
she can't help feeling
still happening
in parallel dimensions

you spurned me before
and i understand
i don't fit the life you're leading
still i'll ask your hand
every then once more
cause you're still the door
on which my heart keeps beating

do you miss life as a real person
cleansed by harmonious nature

she knows she shouldn't
but always revisits
the remnants of love's disasters

IX.
STORIES

IX. STORIES

he loves to walk

on misty days

when sound nor sight

can travel far

and ravens scare

from his heart's bright light

reflecting in feathers of glassy tar

they broke mirrors

for being offensive

and silenced singers

contrasting their crows

locked up stirrers

who made folks pensive

and cut off fingers

denoting their lows

life like a doctor's waiting room
hushed looks
and wondering 'bout
strangers' afflictions
rapt in old gossip
till it's our turn

people call her self-indulgent
but nobody wants to indulge her

no i don't hate you
she answered the stranger
and passing me's
sure to keep it like that

IX. STORIES

the one thing
he wanted her to know
he could not keep himself
taking away
as he sometimes put it
for lack of reward

melody was her name
and like a song
her life ended in refrain

he learned to grasp
the tension of time
from spaces filled with happy

the places he kissed her
in church
seemed improper
but god kept watching them anyway

eating makes her
embrace the earth
but she prefers
numbness of airy hunger

she lights up men
inhales them deeply
ever since
he made her quit smoking

IX. STORIES

she wanted a castle
and that's what she got
beauty with beauty repaid
when she realized
she was merely bought
she knew it was much too late

she hung on my arms
an exhausted cold bird
then i was certain
i'd never dislike her

why were there no
childhood photos of her

she did not know
what he had put to rest
to seem so calm and collected

she swears
she'll keep him in her heart
but he wants to be all over her

he farmed in the valley
wrestling with oxen
plowing the fields
pushing down with his hands
still all he dreamed of
was lifting her up

IX. STORIES

people he knows
walk by like ghosts
they look right through him
or fake not to see
he lives in the past
before he was cast
not useful anymore

nobody said hi
to counter his low

she opened
and asked me
to come inside

sure as she was
a chalice of love
he drank her
and threw her away

no no no no no
she laughs
you go
you go first

a video sees back before she departed
so lifelike it now is hard to bear
he sits in a dark room weary hearted
trying to think of what black to wear

IX. STORIES

she rises his sleep
until he smiles
he puts her to bed
until she sighs
morning and evening persons

the little elf
left her mushroom home
to dance in the fields
and make love to a gnome

malgré cela she somberly whispered
and i thought these words meant
her faith had waned

like a chinchilla
with hidden razors
he would not know
at first when she cut

he screams at her
to go to hell
then realizing
that's where they have been

married a mackerel
or might as well
fortnight passed
she could not stand the smell

IX. STORIES

so cut so blunt and unafraid
of what her judgment would be
the less he cared the more she did
to try to make him see

she admits i must have been crazy
he responds i hope you still are
teases him claiming a little too lazy
i'm not for you like before the war

moorlands cradled her
gardening naked
hares and the postman
kept her secret

baloney baloney
she kept repeating
the worst curse a vegan
like she could cast

his desire to sire
was for hire
but lack of a buyer
had him self-employed

mold covered land
like soft muted blankets
stirred every then
in swirling spores

IX. STORIES

seal in labor complications
pulled herself up on the beach
deadly exhausted
ignored by most
the rest are taking pictures

his decision to stop being cool
cost him dearly with the crowd
her decision to make him her fool
cast him finally down and out

prefers field poppies
over roses
leaving them unplucked

the last move he makes
is his hand on her eyes
so she will not see
how his love for her dies

she was of a dour disposition
and had no taste for sweet
his love seemed an awful imposition
that's why he took refuge in mead

their love story
had reached an impasse
where nothing and everything
needed be said

IX. STORIES

take off those riding
gloves and tights
spring in the spring
and back to life
where under trees
the grass lies waiting

she held his promises dearest
long after they had turned to lies

when someone familiar
entered the room
we detached
as temporary strangers

in a past blooming
of soul to a mind
this child was crushed
digging coal in a mine

as she rescinded
to run after people
much more attention
fell on her path

you'd like me to write
of love and its beauty
but sometimes its want
to mourn is my duty

IX. STORIES

he's a platitudipus
she a philosloth

i knew surfer girls are different
when she said she didn't
own hard shoes

marathon runner
faster than i
did not mind seeing her
from behind
her dog shuttling
gave his acceptance
of my becoming part of the pack

i fell in love with a girl hitchhiker

when she mourned insects

hitting the windshield

she said she lived

where the moon's full and brighter

one more sign she was not from here

she chose to live

like she pictured the afterlife

for undead souls and hopeless sinners

so many suitors

she picked me

even insisting i picked her

IX. STORIES

conjured were
all her spirits and stories

i am a knight
betrothed to the might
of right and principled love
committeed evil
made me an outlaw
forcing me to fight

to foster his path his impulse was
the purchase of a new car
but better by far he invested instead
in travel experiences and a bed

she wakes me up after nightmares
to still her bleeding heart's worries

he marched to the shore
commanding the sea
to swallow him or recede

he keeps repeating
he understands her
however never lets her talk
she keeps fearing
he will blame her
for being a problem
and one day walk

IX. STORIES

she balanced her surf board

like a tray

to indicate what just had happened

in hushed tones

encountering humans can't hear

demons and angels

fight love or hate

one by one deciding our fate

no fairy tale dear is without any fear

or damage that calls for its mending

the story we share lays all of us bare

still let us not cut to an ending

he tried calming her
i will come back
say why she weeped
buried in his neck

to gain familiarity he remarked
that she had amber eyes too
yet this worked against him
implying blood relation

all people he claims
should plan their funerals
at least then they'd know
what they'll be getting

X.
OUT
AND
WITHIN

X. OUT AND WITHIN

the way she cradles
this fallen baby bird
nothing but life
its life
now matters

will we win the day
or dream it away
romantics underestimated

it's not hurt pride
that chills him so
but not being able
to love a foe

going away party

her whole existence

forlorn love born from mourning

abrasions and cuts

you gave me in fights

sorry to bleed all over you

she says i am like an explosion

but that's only when

someone tries to contain me

the why of you

not caring for me

is keeping me endlessly dying

she got her reward

forsaking me waiting

though she never learned

how i writhed inside

feeling no rocks

in our stomachs

basking in love

full of light

and unbound

pieces of unlived life

stacked on my table

soon to be cleared

because i did not dare

your freedom you place

in my hands

to hold for you

your wings brush me gently

expanding my realm

the island i was

on nothing that time

i could have used a friend

X. OUT AND WITHIN

dreaming some day
you'll come my way
or there is a path
by which i will find you
meanwhile i practice
so i can sway
your gentle soul
into loving to stay

soused she doused insistent thoughts
how cruel it is to sell herself

all the interesting people i know
show interest beyond themselves

the rivers of tears

we cry inside

leave our lives

emotional deserts

i know my love

i'm not easy to read

i'm scared you'd be scared

of my inner world

worries and daily drudges

preoccupy her mind

she does not allow herself to shine

only with you some time

X. OUT AND WITHIN

closed in shielding castle walls
withering from within
she asks me where i'm going
not fathoming where i've been

give me this love again
i beg
when i thought
the world would
see it and echo

he had her moods moving
like bodies of water
touched by the shapes of his terrain

malignant they found
is part of her
trying to take over

breaking records of living
with a broken heart

you mock my defenselessness
and put me down
so here's what my
sorrowed love's come to
i'll be your clown until i drown
with ghostly pride
that won't haunt you

X. OUT AND WITHIN

all she wants

is gentle attention

without people seeing

the wounds yet to heal

i once thought to write her

explaining my love

then sensing more deeply

it never would right

waning wanting

now underground

as granular bit storms

are wearing her down

she wanted him always
around and within her
but he felt he needed
somewhat else sometimes

if you show you care
and leave wires bare
someone will come
to cherish their sparkle

two shy people
broaching their bliss
unfit to reign in their feelings
no experience primed them for this

X. OUT AND WITHIN

i love the way
you brighten me
when dark alley walls close in
you say you see
the fight in me
to make compassion win

i will not tell her
she's on my mind
she is much further within

many men vie for superpowers
he's a chap who likes little flowers
and the sun making them come up

her favorite lament
there is nowhere to go
everything's caught
in a screen and a button

every now
i step out of the shadows
that threaten to pull me under

inviting him in
her world
to love her
but not so much
it would crowd her out

X. OUT AND WITHIN

you
through the earth
under the seas
over the skies
i sense you

looking deep into her eyes
she confided i trust you
so close to the mirror
her breath fogged it over

slick body she learned to showcase
as mantle for naked raw feelings
shell-locked like the seed of a fruit

she felt she might as well

live on the moon

with an internet connection

painful though

to keep seeing the earth

numb cringing ringing

and crawling time

set off by inner detonations

whenever she's near but not mine

reaching out

is a good way

for reaching in

www.ingramcontent.com/pod-product-compliance
Lightning Source LLC
Chambersburg PA
CBHW032109090426
42743CB00007B/293